Ozone and Foliar Injury Report for Cumberland Piedmont Network Parks

Annual Report 2008

Natural Resource Data Series NPS/CUPN/NRDS—2009/012

Johnathan Jernigan and Bobby C. Carson

National Park Service
P.O. Box 7
Mammoth Cave, KY 42259

Teresa Leibfreid

National Park Service
P.O. Box 8
Mammoth Cave, KY 42259

November 2009

U.S. Department of the Interior
National Park Service
Natural Resource Program Center
Fort Collins, Colorado

The National Park Service, Natural Resource Program Center publishes a range of reports that address natural resource topics of interest and applicability to a broad audience in the National Park Service and others in natural resource management, including scientists, conservation and environmental constituencies, and the public.

The Natural Resource Data Series is intended for timely release of basic data sets and data summaries. Care has been taken to assure accuracy of raw data values, but a thorough analysis and interpretation of the data has not been completed. Consequently, the initial analyses of data in this report are provisional and subject to change.

All manuscripts in the series receive the appropriate level of peer review to ensure that the information is scientifically credible, technically accurate, appropriately written for the intended audience, and designed and published in a professional manner. Data in this report were collected and analyzed using methods based on established, peer-reviewed protocols and were analyzed and interpreted within the guidelines of the protocols.

Views, statements, findings, conclusions, recommendations, and data in this report are those of the author(s) and do not necessarily reflect views and policies of the National Park Service, U.S. Department of the Interior. Mention of trade names or commercial products does not constitute endorsement or recommendation for use by the National Park Service.

This report is available from the Cumberland Piedmont Network's intranet site (http://www1.nrintra.nps.gov/im/units/CUPN) and the Natural Resource Publications Management website (http://www.nature.nps.gov/publications/NRPM).

Please cite this publication as:

Jernigan, J. W., B. Carson, and T. Leibfreid. 2009. Ozone and foliar injury report for Cumberland Piedmont Network parks: Annual report 2008. Natural Resource Data Series NPS/CUPN/NRDS—2009/012. National Park Service, Fort Collins, Colorado.

NPS 910/100711, November 2009

Contents

Figures

Tables

Abstract

This is the Cumberland Piedmont Network's (CUPN's) first annual report on ozone levels and associated foliar injury at its parks. The time period covered by this report is 2008 and the parks at which data were collected are Abraham Lincoln Birthplace NHP (ABLI), Cumberland Gap NHP (CUGA) and Mammoth Cave NP (MACA). Ozone level/foliar injury data and associated analyses are presented for each of the three parks listed. Further, summary statistics of ozone level data from off-park state-operated monitors are presented for the remaining CUPN parks.

Acknowledgments

The investigators would like to thank park staff at ABLI, CUGA and MACA for their assistance. In particular, thanks to Sandy Brue at ABLI, Jenny Beeler at CUGA and CUGA SCA's Amanda Deeds and Lindsay Nystrom for helping with the foliar injury assessments at each of their parks. We would also like to thank CUPN staff at the MACA office (Sammi Jo Doyle, Lillian Scoggins and Brenda Wells) for their assistance.

Introduction

This is the first report on ozone and its associated foliar impacts generated by the Cumberland Piedmont Network (CUPN). This report includes those data collected in FY2008 and displays these results in tabular and graphic form (accompanied with a brief interpretation), and concludes with a summary of the key results and recommendations. The CUPN's ozone and foliar injury efforts in FY2008 were focused on three parks: Mammoth Cave NP (MACA), Abraham Lincoln Birthplace NHP (ABLI) and Cumberland Gap NHP (CUGA). Results presented in this report are primarily based on data collected at these three parks.

Ozone level data were collected at only two of the three primary parks in FY2008. One of those sites was the Portable Ozone Monitoring Station (POMS) that is located in CUGA. The site has been operated jointly by CUGA staff and National Park Service – Air Resources Division (NPS-ARD). This report contains results from the analyses of data from that site. Additionally, MACA, working cooperatively with NPS-ARD, services and maintains its own ozone monitoring site, and detailed analyses of those data will be presented in this report. Lastly, no ozone level data were collected at an ABLI site in FY2008. However, past analyses by the authors indicated that ozone level data collected at the nearby Elizabethtown, KY site can be used to approximate, with limited confidence, the magnitude of ozone levels at ABLI. Because the authors have no on-park data to use, limited analyses of the Elizabethtown data will be used to suggest an explanation for the results of the foliar injury survey at ABLI. Details of the aforementioned past data analyses may be found in the CUPN Ozone and Foliar Injury protocol available by contacting the authors or, for NPS personnel, at http://www1.nrintra.nps.gov/im/monitor/VitalSignsDB/BrowseProtocol.aspx.

For the eleven remaining CUPN parks, ozone level data from one nearby, state-operated site are presented for each park (just as data from Elizabethtown are presented for ABLI). The results of these analyses apply only to the state-operated site from which they were collected, and not directly to the park with which they are paired. These analyses are presented only in order to provide these remaining CUPN parks with an index of cumulative ozone levels.

Foliar injury data were collected at three parks in FY2008: ABLI, CUGA and MACA. At ABLI, three sites were surveyed for foliar injury, while at CUGA there were two sites and at MACA there was one site. An example of a damaged leaf is shown in Figure 1.

Figure 1 – A damaged milkweed leaf from MACA.

Sampling Sites

ABLI Visitor Center (ABLI-01-Foln)

The ABLI Visitor Center area is located near the town of Hodgenville, KY. The area is in an urban area and is roughly bisected by a major highway. Plants were sampled in each of the area's halves. Plants within 100 feet of the road were not considered per the requirements of the US Forest Service protocol, upon which the CUPN foliar injury sampling approach is closely based. The elevation of the site is about 760 feet.

Figure 2 – ABLI Visitor Center area site photographs and maps.

ABLI Knob Creek Low Field (ABLI-02-FoIn)

The Knob Creek unit (currently known as the Abraham Lincoln Boyhood Home at Knob Creek unit) of ABLI is to the northeast of the Visitor Center unit. The site photo shows the boyhood home off in the distance. This building is on the eastern boundary of the unit and is adjacent to a major highway. The Knob Creek Low Field site is in a low-lying field. Plants were sampled along the forest edge shown on the left of the photo. A small stream also runs along this edge and plants from the open sections of the stream were also sampled. The forest edge on the right was not sampled since that edge is north-facing and does not receive direct sunlight. The elevation of the site is 570 feet.

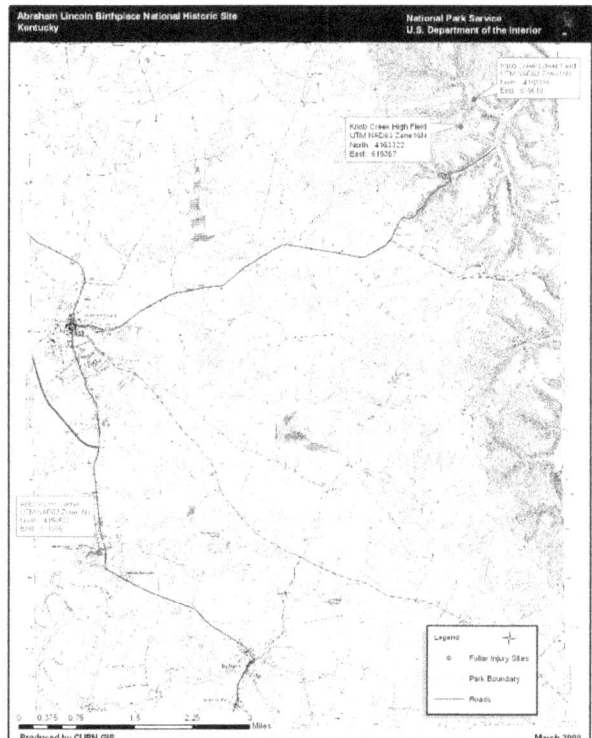

Figure 3 – ABLI Knob Creek Low site photograph and maps.

ABLI Knob Creek High Field (ABLI-03-FoIn)

The Knob Creek High Field is a small field on the top of a hill that lies off to the right edge of the ABLI-02 site photo. Plants were sampled along the edges of and inside the field. With an elevation of 810 feet, the high field site is higher in elevation than the low field site.

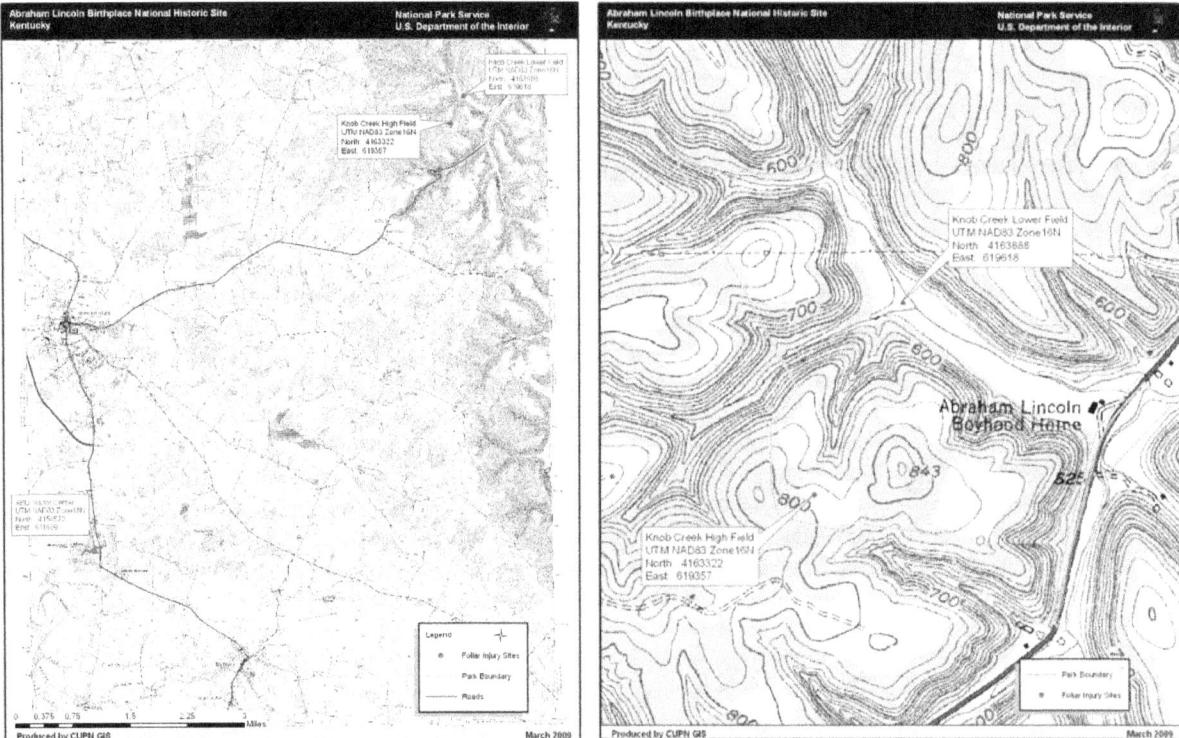

Figure 4 – ABLI Knob Creek High site photograph and maps.

CUGA Daniel Boone Trail (CUGA-01-Foln)

The CUGA Daniel Boone Trail is a low-elevation site located along the Daniel Boone Trail. Plants were selected beginning at the patch of common milkweed shown in the foreground right of the site photo and extending slightly beyond the patch of sycamore trees that cross the clearing off in the distance. The site map is courtesy of CUGA staff. The leftmost green dot is the Daniel Boone Trail. The elevation of the site is about 1,300 feet.

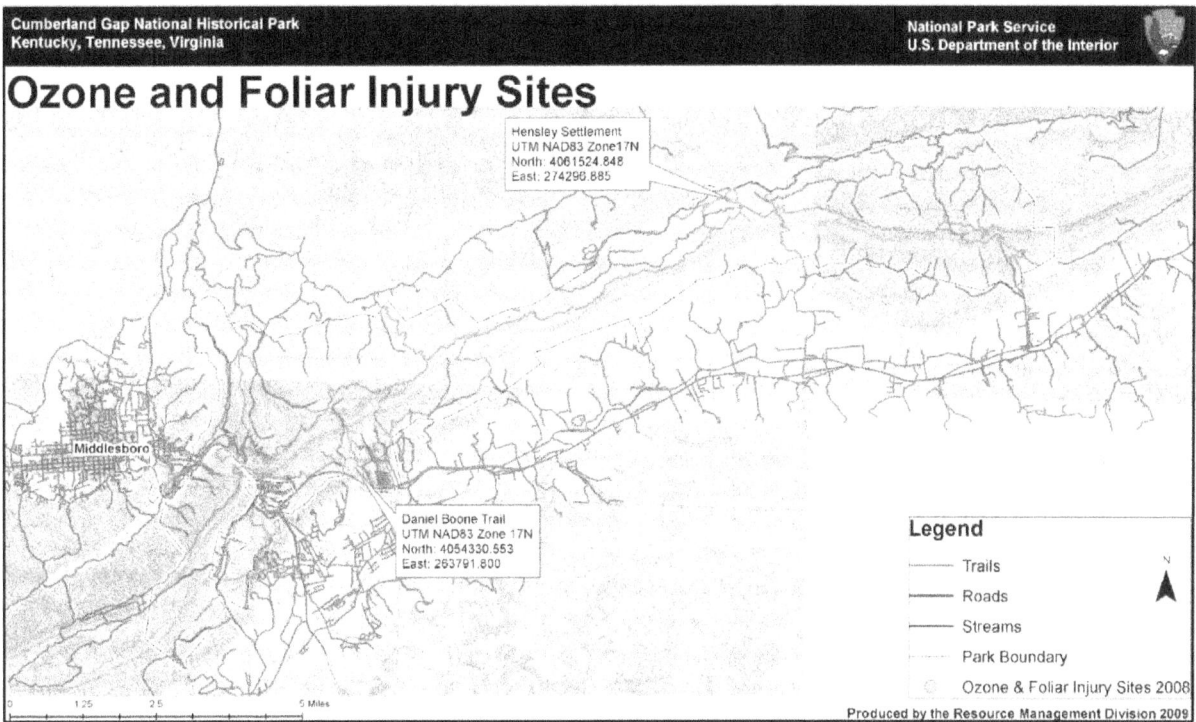

Figure 5 - CUGA Daniel Boone Trail site photograph and map. Map courtesy CUGA staff.

CUGA Hensley Settlement (CUGA-02-Foln/OL)

The Hensley Settlement site at CUGA is the site of both a foliar injury assessment and the NPS-ARD/CUGA operated POMS. The POMS is located away from the edge of the field. Foliar injury sampling was conducted by looking at plants along the edge of and throughout the opening. The Hensley Settlement is a high elevation site. The site photo is a general photo provided by CUGA staff and was taken by John Graves. The elevation of the site is about 3,330 feet.

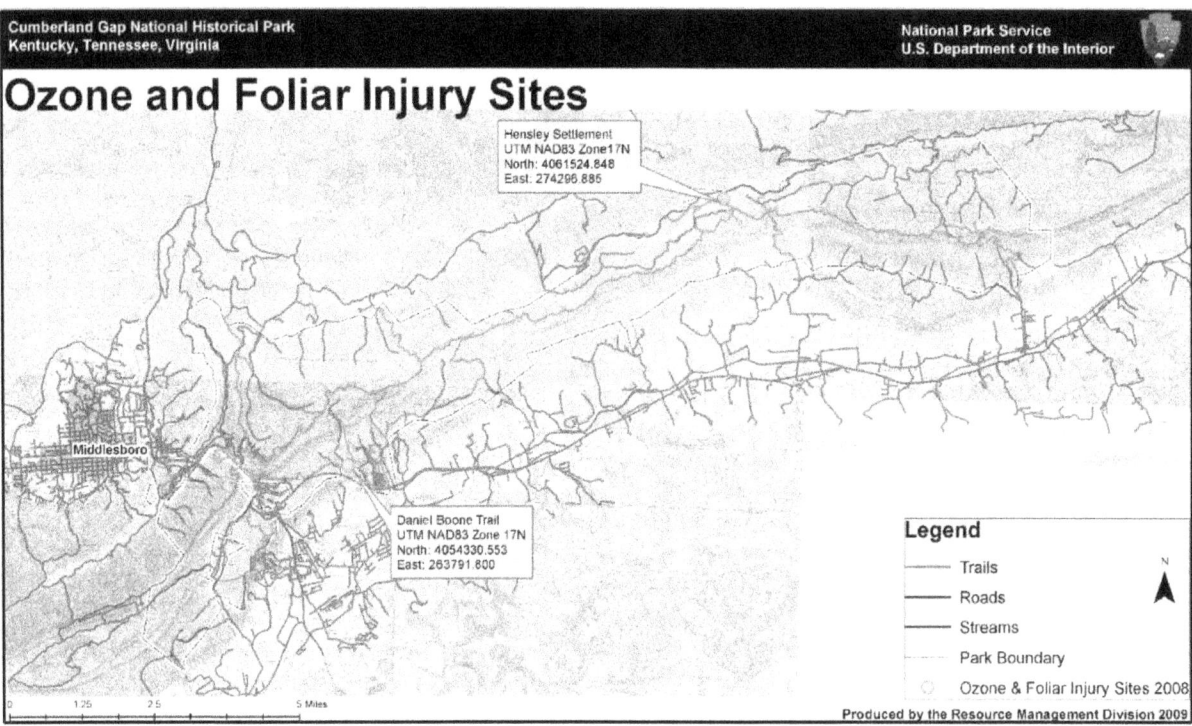

Figure 6 – CUGA Hensley Settlement site photograph and map. Map courtesy CUGA staff. Photo by John Graves.

MACA Great Onyx Job Corps (MACA-01-FoIn)

MACA's Great Onyx Job Corps site lies on the northwest corner of the park. The 2008 foliar injury sampling was conducted by US Forest Service personnel as part of a training course for NPS personnel who would be taking part in the upcoming assessments at ABLI and CUGA. Plants were sampled from within the large opening, not from along its edges. The site photograph is a generic photograph of the Great Onyx Job Corps and does not show the particular location where sampling was completed in 2008. The elevation of the site is about 650 feet.

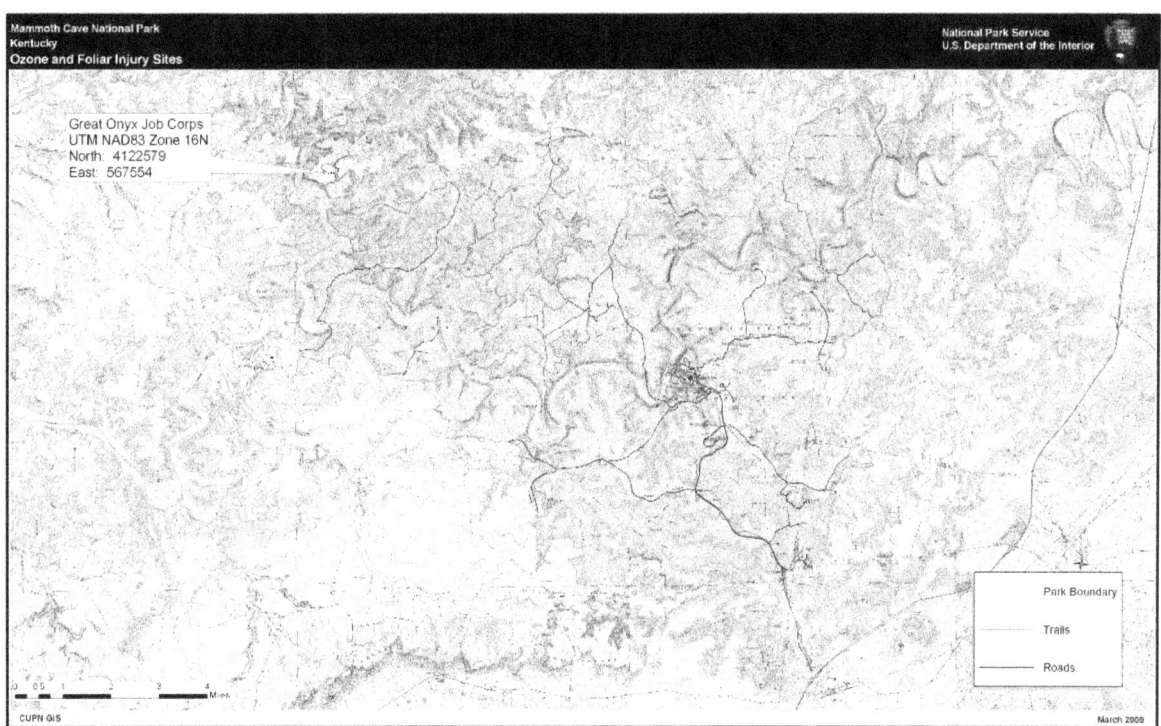

Figure 7 – MACA Great Onyx Job Corps site photograph and map.

MACA Air Quality Station (MACA-02-OL)

MACA's air quality station lies on the western boundary of the park. The only sampling done at this site is for ozone levels; no foliar injury sampling was completed. The site's ozone analyzer is an EPA-equivalent method and the site's data are of sufficient quality to be used for permit review. The analyzer is housed in the leftmost and largest building, near the center of the photograph. At the rear of that building is a tower and at the top of the tower is an inlet through which air is drawn for the analyzer. There are three towers in the photograph; the tower mentioned is the middle tower.

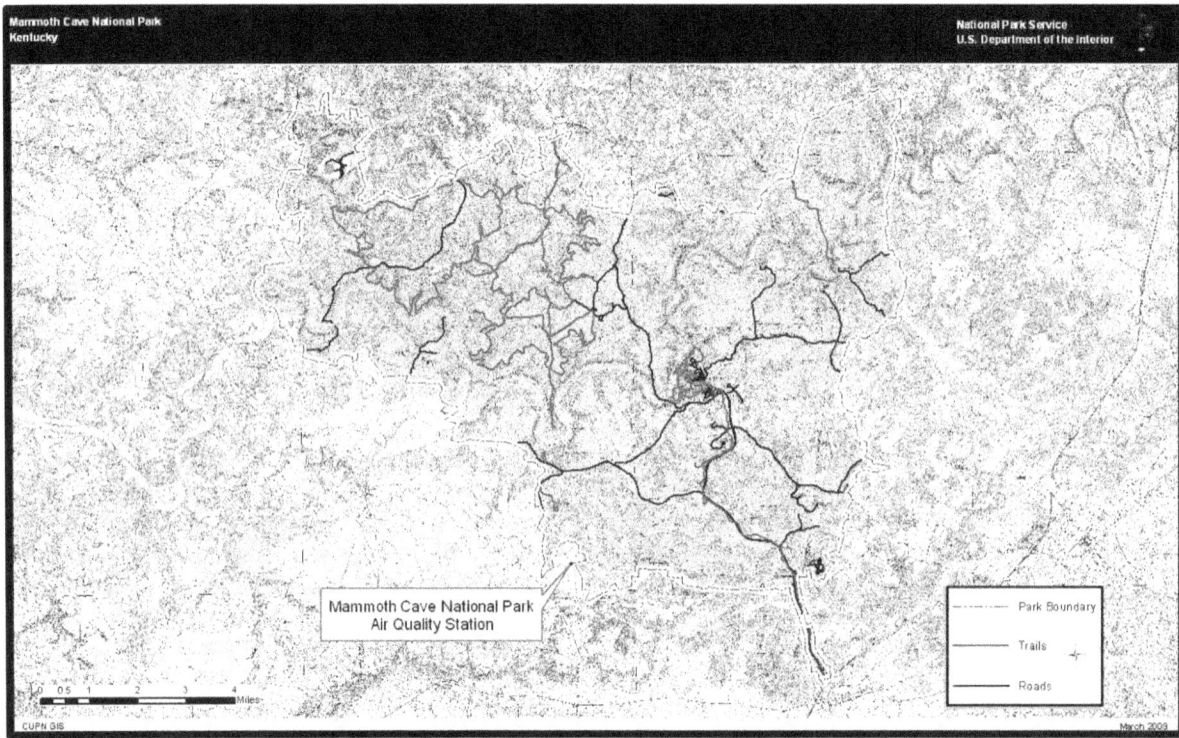

Figure 8 – MACA Air Quality Station site photograph and map.

Results

The CUPN has mined ozone level data from external sources for those parks at which foliar injury sampling was conducted. Foliar injury assessments were conducted by the CUPN for a total of six sites spread across three parks in FY2008. The three parks and their ozone level data sources are:

- ABLI – Ozone level data are from a state-operated site in Elizabethtown, Kentucky.
- CUGA – Ozone level data are from a Portable Ozone Monitoring Station (POMS) located at CUGA's Hensley Settlement.
- MACA – Ozone level data are from the park's air quality station located along the park's eastern boundary.

Ozone Levels

Ozone level data are displayed in time series graphs and one scatterplot. Three time series plots are shown for each of the ozone level sites. The first plot shows all available ozone level data for the entire ozone season. The second plot shows all available ozone level data for the ozone season up to the time of the foliar injury assessment. This second plot provides information on conditions prior to the foliar injury assessment. The third time series plot is a subset of the previous plots, showing only seven days of data. Viewing the data in this way allows one to determine whether there are diurnal fluctuations at the site of interest. Generally and for no particular reason, the seven day period immediately prior to the foliar injury assessment is shown. A scatterplot is also shown in which the entire season's available ozone data are plotted against the hour during which they were collected. This also allows the exploration of the existence of diurnal fluctuations.

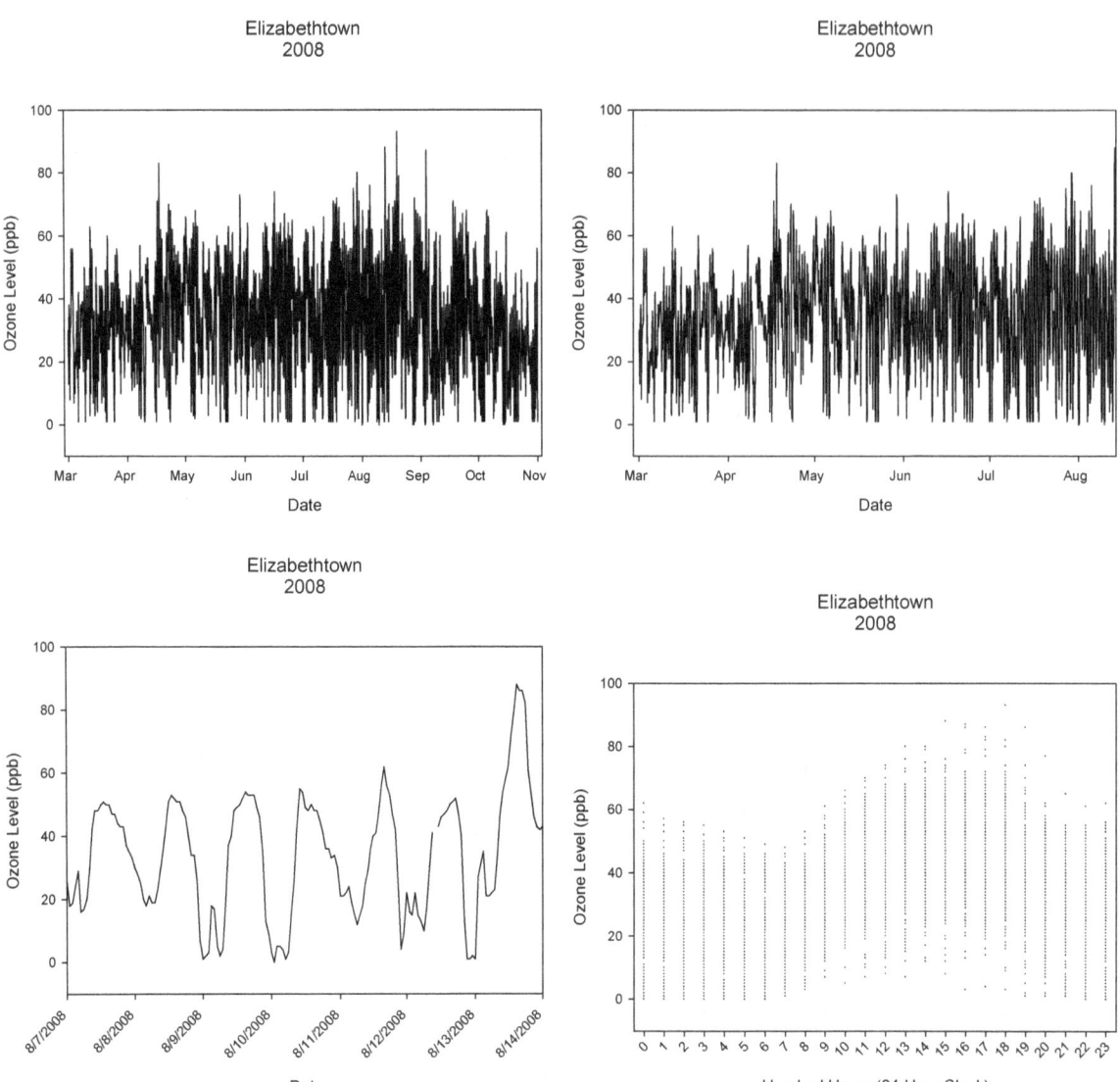

Figure 9 – Elizabethtown (ABLI substitute) ozone level plots.

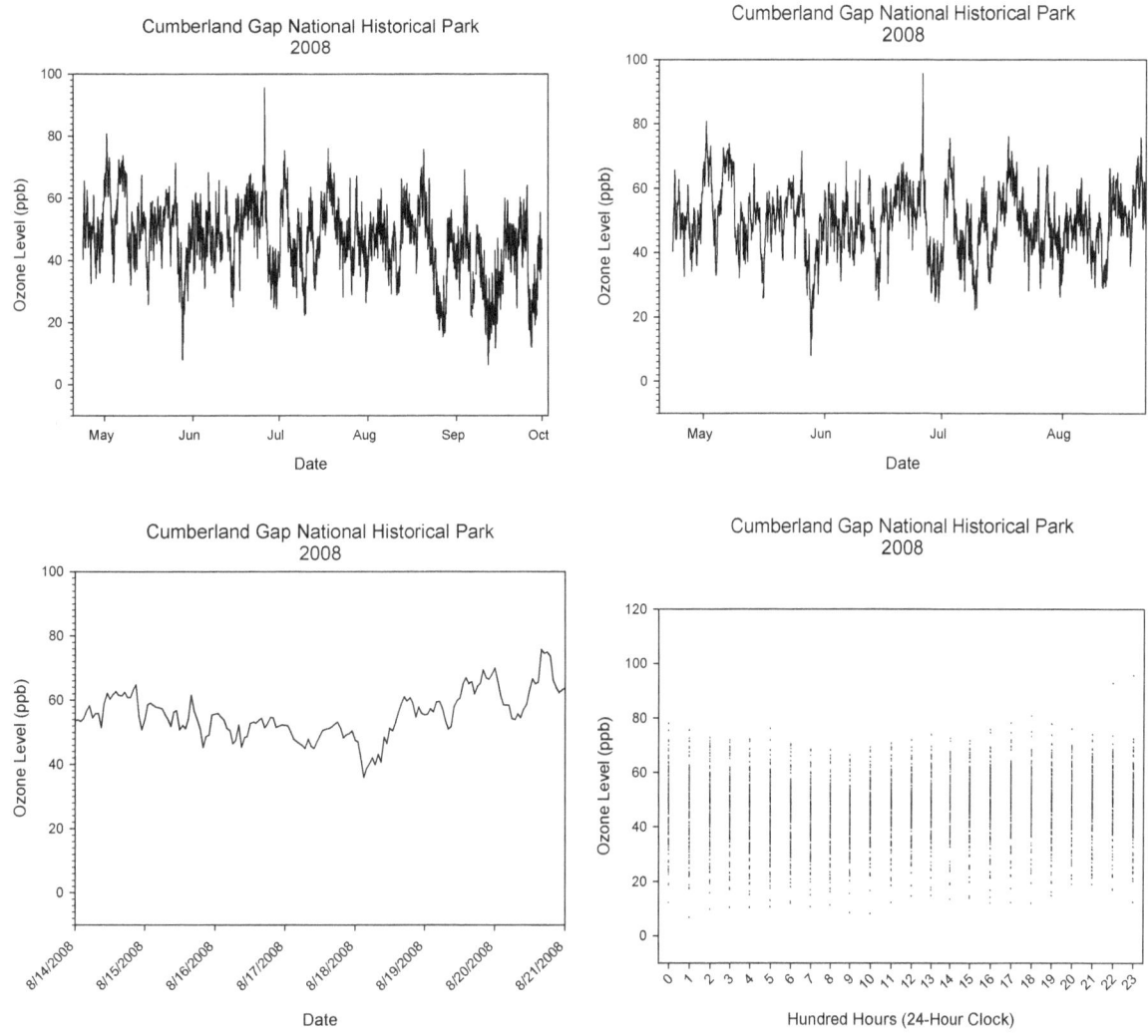

Figure 10 – CUGA ozone level plots

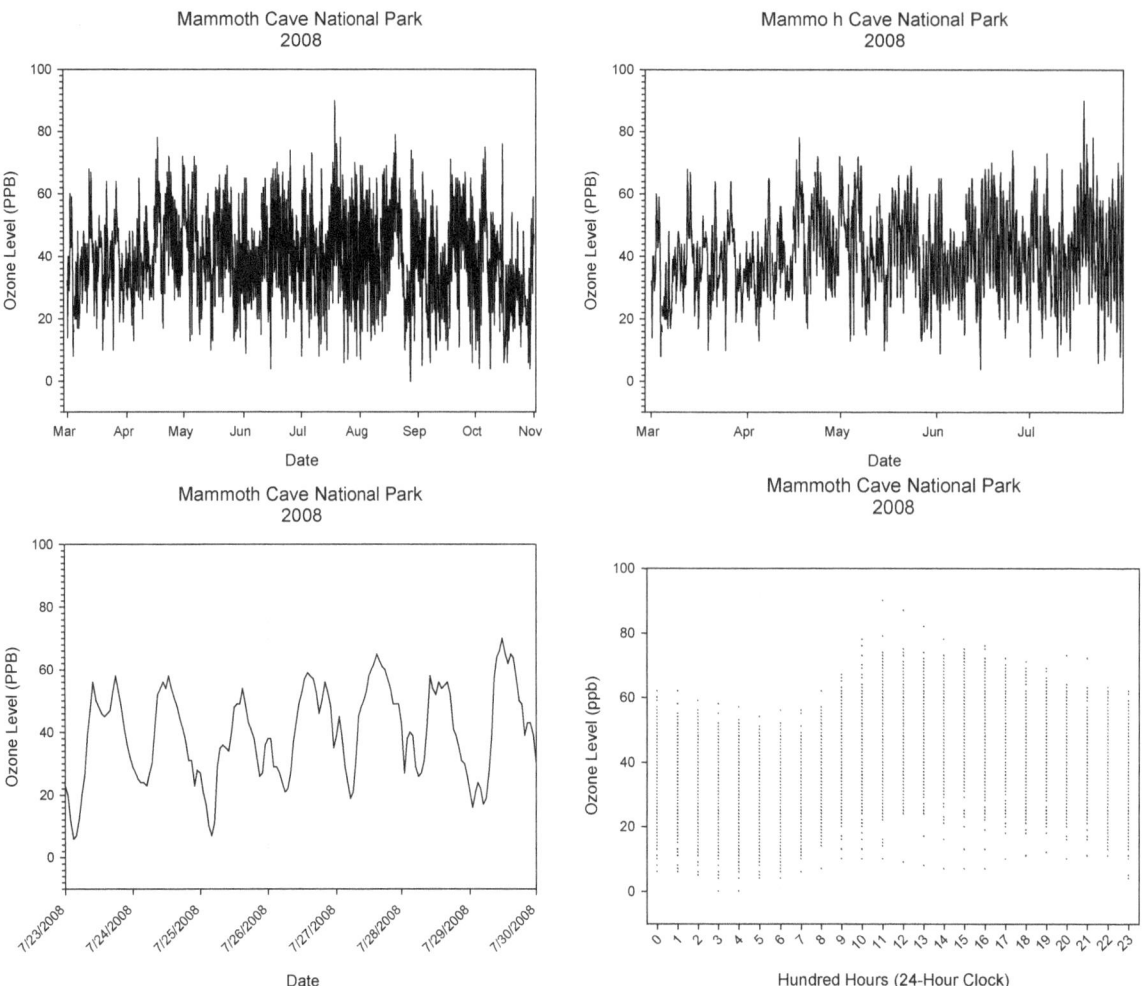

Figure 11 – MACA ozone level plots.

There are several metrics available to ascertain whether the ozone levels seen in the time series plots mentioned above are considered to be too high. The current standard for ozone levels as set by the Environmental Protection Agency (EPA) is that the eight hour average should not exceed 0.075 ppm. Currently, that value is the primary (human health) standard as well as the secondary (public welfare) standard. It is the public welfare standard that is applied to non-human health issues such as ozone sensitive plants. The EPA has set such standards to allow the determination of whether current levels are having detrimental effects on the targeted group. In the case of plant welfare, scientists generally agree that the secondary standard is not the best measure. One of two alternative statistics is generally used: the SUM06 or the W126. In this report, the W126 will not be used, and so it will not be discussed here. The SUM06 is the seasonal running sum of all hourly ozone level measurements above 60 ppb, usually expressed as ppm-hours. The SUM06 is considered a better statistic for plant welfare because it is cumulative and emphasizes the effects of higher ozone levels. Sensitivity to ozone varies amongst species, but SUM06 values in the 8-12 ppm-hrs range are the values that can produce foliar injury in natural ecosystems. The SUM06 values for ABLI, CUGA and MACA are given in Table 1.

Table 1 – SUM06 values for ABLI, CUGA and MACA.

Park Name	Data Source	SUM06 in 2008 Ozone Season (ppm-hrs)	SUM06 at Time of Foliar Injury Surveys (ppm-hrs)	SUM06 Exceeds 8-12 ppm-hrs (Y/N)
ABLI	Elizabethtown State Site	26	17	Y
CUGA	POMS at Hensley Settlement Site	34 (based on partial data set)	32 (based on partial data set)	Y
MACA	Houchins' Meadows Site	37	23	Y

Foliar Injury

In FY2008, foliar injury assessments were completed at three parks on the indicated dates:

Abraham Lincoln Birthplace National Historical Park – August 14, 2008
Cumberland Gap National Historical Park – August 21, 2008
Mammoth Cave National Park – July 30, 2008

Foliar injury assessments are conducted by visually inspecting plant leaves for ozone damage and noting presence/absence of the damage on a field form. In those cases where damage is found, three injured leaves are collected for each species. These injured leaves (referred to as voucher specimens) are preserved and later sent to a regional expert on ozone damage. The regional expert will provide a second opinion on the damage seen on the voucher specimens. The damage will either be confirmed or not confirmed by the regional expert. If the damage is not confirmed by the regional expert, the CUPN does not consider plants from that park/site/species to be positive for ozone damage.

Table 2 – List of plants with confirmed and unconfirmed foliar injury.

Park Name	Injury Confirmed (Y/N)	Date	Site Name	Species	Amount	Severity	Plant Number
MACA	Y	7/30/2008	Job Corps	Tulip Poplar	1	1	2
MACA	Y	7/30/2008	Job Corps	Common Milkweed	2	2	28
MACA	Y	7/30/2008	Job Corps	Common Milkweed	1	1	27
MACA	Y	7/30/2008	Job Corps	Common Milkweed	1	1	26
MACA	Y	7/30/2008	Job Corps	Common Milkweed	1	1	25
CUGA	Y	8/21/2008	Hensley Settlement	Sassafras	1	1	21
CUGA	Y	8/21/2008	Hensley Settlement	Sassafras	2	3	1
MACA	N	7/30/2008	Job Corps	Ash	1	1	1
MACA	N	7/30/2008	Job Corps	Sweet Gum	1	2	12
ABLI	N	8/14/2008	Top Field	Ash	5	4	30
ABLI	N	8/14/2008	Top Field	Ash	2	4	21
ABLI	N	8/14/2008	Knob Creek	Blackberry	1	3	1
ABLI	N	8/14/2008	Knob Creek	Tulip Poplar	1	2	9
ABLI	N	8/14/2008	Birthplace	White Ash	1	2	17
ABLI	N	8/14/2008	Birthplace	White Ash	2	1	1

There was confirmed foliar injury at CUGA and MACA (seven plants total from confirmed park/site/species), but not ABLI. There were eight plants from unconfirmed park/site/species (several species from ABLI and MACA). The one species at CUGA with observed injury was confirmed by lab inspection of voucher samples. Table 2 summarizes these results.

Table 3 – Total number of plants inspected at each of the CUPN parks.

Park Name	Number of Plants Inspected
ABLI	370
CUGA	227
MACA	125
Total	722

In FY2008, 722 plants at three CUPN parks were inspected for foliar injury. Of those 722 plants, there were seven plants from confirmed park/site/species. Table 3 shows the total number of plants inspected at each park. Table 4 further breaks down the information in Table 3 by showing the number of plants in each park/species. From the table, one may count the number of species inspected at each of the three parks (ABLI had 12 species, CUGA had 10 species, and MACA had 7 species).

Table 4 – Total number of plants per species inspected at each park.

Park Name	Species	Number of Plants Inspected
ABLI	Ash	43
ABLI	Black Cherry	43
ABLI	Black Locust	9
ABLI	Blackberry	9
ABLI	Common Milkweed	6
ABLI	Dogbane	17
ABLI	Redbud	78
ABLI	Sassafras	30
ABLI	Sycamore	30
ABLI	Tulip Poplar	74
ABLI	Virginia Creeper	1
ABLI	White Ash	30
CUGA	Ash	7
CUGA	Black Cherry	7
CUGA	Black Locust	30
CUGA	Common Milkweed	30
CUGA	Dogbane	30
CUGA	Redbud	8
CUGA	Sassafras	30
CUGA	Sweet Gum	5
CUGA	Sycamore	30
CUGA	Tulip Poplar	50
MACA	Ash	2
MACA	Black Cherry	11
MACA	Blackberry	30
MACA	Common Milkweed	30
MACA	Dogbane	30
MACA	Sweet Gum	20
MACA	Tulip Poplar	2

Table 5 summarizes data at the park/site/species level. The number of plants from each species examined at each site is shown. The rightmost column shows whether plants observed to have foliar injury in the field were verified as having ozone injury by the regional expert. If the field-observed injury was verified by the regional expert, the number of plants observed in the field to have ozone-induced foliar injury is shown in square brackets.

14

Table 5 – Plant counts with and without injury sorted by location and species.

Park Name	Site Name	Species	Number of Plants Inspected	Injury Confirmed (Y/N) [Number of Plants with Observed Injury]
ABLI	Birthplace	Black Cherry	29	N
ABLI	Birthplace	Blackberry	7	N
ABLI	Birthplace	Redbud	30	N
ABLI	Birthplace	Sassafras	30	N
ABLI	Birthplace	Tulip Poplar	14	N
ABLI	Birthplace	White Ash	30	N
ABLI	Knob Creek	Ash	13	N
ABLI	Knob Creek	Black Cherry	14	N
ABLI	Knob Creek	Black Locust	9	N
ABLI	Knob Creek	Blackberry	2	N
ABLI	Knob Creek	Redbud	30	N
ABLI	Knob Creek	Sycamore	30	N
ABLI	Knob Creek	Tulip Poplar	30	N
ABLI	Knob Creek	Virginia Creeper	1	N
ABLI	Top Field	Ash	30	N
ABLI	Top Field	Common Milkweed	6	N
ABLI	Top Field	Dogbane	17	N
ABLI	Top Field	Redbud	18	N
ABLI	Top Field	Tulip Poplar	30	N
CUGA	Daniel Boone Trail	Ash	7	N
CUGA	Daniel Boone Trail	Black Cherry	1	N
CUGA	Daniel Boone Trail	Common Milkweed	30	N
CUGA	Daniel Boone Trail	Redbud	8	N
CUGA	Daniel Boone Trail	Sweet Gum	5	N
CUGA	Daniel Boone Trail	Sycamore	30	N
CUGA	Daniel Boone Trail	Tulip Poplar	30	N
CUGA	Hensley Settlement	Black Cherry	6	N
CUGA	Hensley Settlement	Black Locust	30	N
CUGA	Hensley Settlement	Dogbane	30	N
CUGA	Hensley Settlement	Sassafras	30	Y[2]
CUGA	Hensley Settlement	Tulip Poplar	20	N
MACA	Job Corps	Ash	2	N
MACA	Job Corps	Black Cherry	11	N
MACA	Job Corps	Blackberry	30	N
MACA	Job Corps	Common Milkweed	30	Y[4]
MACA	Job Corps	Dogbane	30	N
MACA	Job Corps	Sweet Gum	20	N
MACA	Job Corps	Tulip Poplar	2	Y[1]

The Interrelationship of Ozone Levels and Drought Severity with Foliar Injury

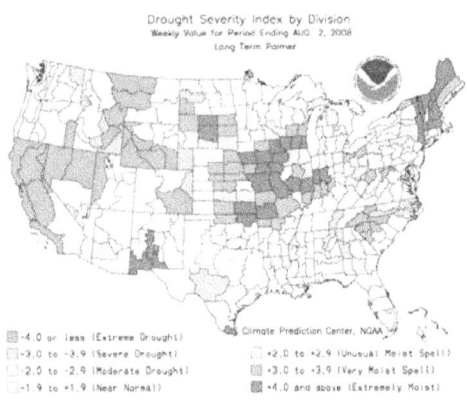

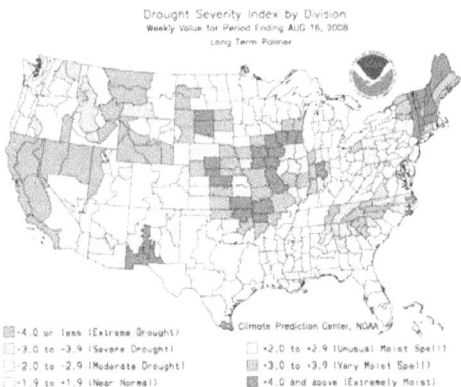

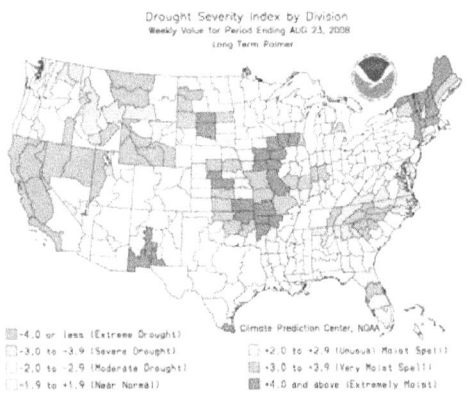

http://www.cpc.ncep.noaa.gov/products/MD_in
dex.shtml

Figure 12 - Drought severity index maps for
CUPN parks during foliar injury assessments.

Excessively dry conditions can cause plants to reduce their level of activity. This reduction results in less gas exchange across the plant's leaf surface through its stomata (the "pores" of the plant leaf). Plants are therefore somewhat less susceptible to high ozone levels during times of drought because ozone is not coming into contact with the cell walls of the leaf.

The plots on the left show the drought severity at the time of the foliar injury assessment for each of the parks sampled. Those parks are, from top to bottom, MACA, ABLI and CUGA. Notice that neither MACA nor ABLI are under drought conditions. CUGA, however, is under a moderate drought.

Ozone levels at ABLI were sufficient to cause damage to only the most sensitive plants (the SUM06 at the time of the foliar injury assessment was 17 ppm-hrs). This low SUM06 is the likely reason for no confirmed foliar injury being found.

The limited injury noticed at CUGA (two sassafras trees showed confirmed injury) may have been a result of the combination of somewhat dry conditions and moderate ozone levels. Further, these plants were located at the higher elevation Hensley Settlement, whose ozone level plots have already been presented. Recall the lack of diurnal cycling at the site. So, many of the higher ozone readings were taken at night when plants are not active and so were not susceptible to the higher ozone concentrations much of the time. However, it is possible that, for both CUGA sites (Hensley and Daniel Boone Tr.), had CUGA not been under a moderate drought, more foliar injury would have been found.

MACA was not in a drought, so lack of moisture should not have been a factor. Recall that four common milkweed plants and one tulip poplar showed confirmed ozone injury. The SUM06 at the time of the injury assessment was 23 ppm-hrs, and this exposure to ozone is sufficient to cause ozone damage to sensitive plants such as common milkweed.

Ozone Levels Near the Remaining CUPN Parks

The CUPN conducted no ozone level or foliar injury monitoring at the eleven remaining CUPN parks. Instead, we have presented in Table 6 the SUM06 of a state-operated site near each of the parks. The nearby sites used in the table are based on the CUPN's 2005 correlation analysis of POMS data collected on each park with multiple nearby sites. The nearby site with the best correlation was considered the best site upon which to base the park's ozone exposure. Where possible, the nearby sites in Table 6 are the best sites based on the 2005 study. If 2008 data are unavailable for the best site, the next best site is used. FODO had only one possible best site in 2005 and that site has also been removed so no 2008 data are available.

It should be noted that the data in Table 6 are presented only to suggest the kinds of ozone levels to which a park may have been exposed in 2008.

Table 6 – Table of CUPN parks and SUM06 for monitors near each park.

Park Name	FIPS of Nearby Site	County, State of Nearby Site	2008 Growing Season SUM06 at Nearby Site (ppm-hr)	SUM06 Exceeds 8-12 ppm-hrs?
CARL	370210030	Buncombe County, NC	23	Yes
CHCH	130550001	Chattooga County, GA	20	Yes
COWP	450210002	Cherokee County, SC	32	Yes
FODO	N/A	N/A	N/A	N/A
GUCO	371570099	Rockingham County, NC	36	Yes
KIMO	450910006	York County, SC	33	Yes
LIRI	130550001	Chattooga County, GA	20	Yes
NISI	450010001	Abbeville County, SC	32	Yes
RUCA	470654003	Hamilton County, TN	39	Yes
SHIL	280810005	Lee County, MS	11	No
STRI	471490101	Rutherford County, TN	29	Yes

General Ozone Level and Foliar Injury Status

At the three sampled parks in 2008, confirmed foliar injury was limited and mild. These findings are consistent with the moderate ozone levels measured under normal drought severity (except at CUGA, where the drought severity was moderate).

Future Ozone and Foliar Injury Monitoring Recommendations

The CUPN monitors ozone and foliar injury according to the schedule established in its ozone level and foliar injury monitoring protocol. That schedule is presented in Table 7. According to that schedule, ABLI, CUGA and MACA will not have CUPN sponsored ozone level monitoring or foliar injury assessments until 2014. MACA maintains its own ozone level monitor, so ozone levels will be monitored by MACA staff during the interim years. As of the time of this report, CUGA has a POMS at the Hensley Settlement that is being provided by NPS-ARD and is being serviced by CUGA staff. That monitoring will continue as long as NPS-ARD staff and CUGA

17

staff are willing to dedicate the resources necessary to maintain the site. The CUPN's monitoring efforts during those interim years will focus on its remaining parks.

Table 7 – CUPN's ozone and foliar injury monitoring schedule.

Park	Year 1 (2008)	Year 2 (2009)	Year 3 (2010)	Year 4 (2011)	Year 5 (2012)	Year 6 (2013)
ABLI	OL, FoIn	--	--	--	--	--
CUGA	OL, FoIn	OL	OL	OL	OL	OL
MACA	FoIn	--	--	--	--	--
FODO	--	OL, FoIn	--	--	--	--
SHIL	--	OL, FoIn	--	--	--	--
COWP	--	FoIn	--	--	--	--
CHCH	--	--	OL, FoIn	--	--	--
STRI	--	--	OL, FoIn	--	--	--
LIRI	--	--	--	OL, FoIn	--	--
RUCA	--	--	--	OL, FoIn	--	--
CARL	--	--	--	--	OL, FoIn	--
GUCO	--	--	--	--	OL, FoIn	--
KIMO	--	--	--	--	--	OL, FoIn
NISI	--	--	--	--	--	OL, FoIn

www.ingramcontent.com/pod-product-compliance
Lightning Source LLC
Chambersburg PA
CBHW081153290526
45795CB00008B/2905